My First Picture Encyclopedia

Show Me
THE
UNITED
STATES

by Patricia Wooster

Consultant:

John Fraser Hart, PhD

Professor, Geography Department

University of Minnesota

CAPSTONE PRESS

a capstone imprint

A+ Books are published by Capstone Press,
1710 Roe Crest Drive, North Mankato, Minnesota 56003.
www.capstonepub.com

Library of Congress Cataloging-in-Publication Data
Wooster, Patricia.
Show me the United States : my first picture encyclopedia / by Patricia Wooster.pages cm.
— (A+. My first picture encyclopedias)
Includes bibliographical references.
ISBN 978-1-4765-0117-8 (library binding)
ISBN 978-1-4765-3347-6 (paper over board)
ISBN 978-1-4765-3351-3 (paperback)
ISBN 978-1-4765-3355-1 (ebook PDF)
1. United States—Encyclopedias, Juvenile. I. Title.
E156.W66 2014
973.03—dc23   2013008520

Editor's Note: All population data was taken from the U.S. Census Bureau:
www.census.gov.

Editorial Credits
Shelly Lyons, editor; Heidi Thompson, designer; Svetlana Zhurkin, media researcher;
Laura Manthe, production specialist

Photo Credits
Dreamstime: Americanspirit, 9 (middle), 27 (middle), Elegeyda, 21 (middle); iStockphotos: Aimin Tang, 30 (top
left), laflor, 8 (left), Nicole S. Young, cover (bottom middle); Library of Congress, 7 (top); Mammoth Cave National
Park Service: Vickie Carson, 31 (middle); Newscom: Andre Jenny Stock Connection Worldwide, 26 (left), KRT/Tom
Uhlenbrock, 26 (right); Robesus, 28, 29; Shutterstock: Achim Baque, 13 (top), Alexey Stiop, 22 (left), Atlaspix, 28
(Georgia state flag), Barry Blackburn, 21 (top), Boykov, 8 (right), Brandon Blinkenberg, 31 (top), Bryan Brazil, 15
(bottom), Bryan Busovicki, 25 (top), Chad Bontrager, 27 (top right), Christopher Halloran, 10, Dan Thornberg
(flag), cover, back cover, 1, Digital Media Pro, 9 (top), Dmitri Ogleznev, 23 (top), Edwin Verin, cover (top right),
1 (top right), 24 (left), Eric Broder Van Dyke, 14 (left), Eric Isselee, back cover (top right), 7 (left), Erika Cross, 11
(middle), FloridaStock, cover (middle left), Fotana (torn paper), cover, 1, iofoto, 14 (right), J. Bicking, back cover
(bottom), July Flower, 18 (bottom), Kasia, cover (bottom right), 7 (middle right), Kenny Tong, 25 (middle), Kim
Seidl, cover (bottom left), Lori Martin, 27 (bottom), Mark Van Dyke Photography, 17 (middle), Mike Flippo, 30
(bottom), Minerva Studio, 20 (left), Natchapon L., 25 (bottom), Orhan Cam, 9 (bottom), Pavelk, 18 (top), Peder
Digre, 17 (top), Peter Kunasz, 16 (left), Ramunas Bruzas, 30 (top right), Rick Laverty, 23 (middle), Robert
Gubbins, 22 (right), Robert Kyllo, 19 (middle), Robynrg, 23 (bottom), Ryan DeBerardinis, 16 (right), S. Borisov,
6, SeDmi (coal), 15, spirit of america, 11 (top), 27 (top left), Steffen Foerster (gold), 15, Thomas Barrat, 31
(right), Tomaj Szymanski, 20 (right), topseller, 24 (right), Vadim Kozlovsky, 19 (top), Vladislav Gurfinkel, 21
(bottom), Volina, 4–5, 12–13, Zelenskaya (copper), 15; The White House: Lawrence Jackson, 11 (bottom)

Note to Parents, Teachers, and Librarians
My First Picture Encyclopedias provide an early introduction to reference materials for young
children. These accessible, visual encyclopedias support literacy development by building
subject-specific vocabularies and research skills. Stimulating format, inviting content, and
phonetic aids assist and encourage young readers.

Printed in the United States of America in North Mankato, Minnesota.
032013   007223CGF13

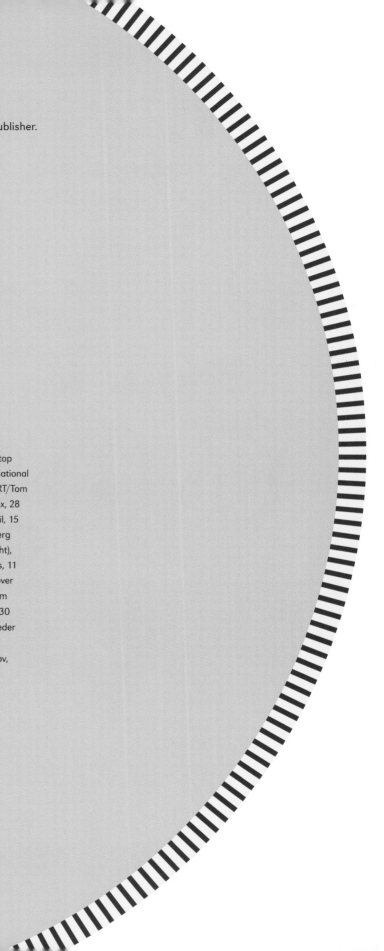

Table of Contents

50 Fabulous States

The United States of America has 50 states. With so many different states to explore, the United States is a great place to live!

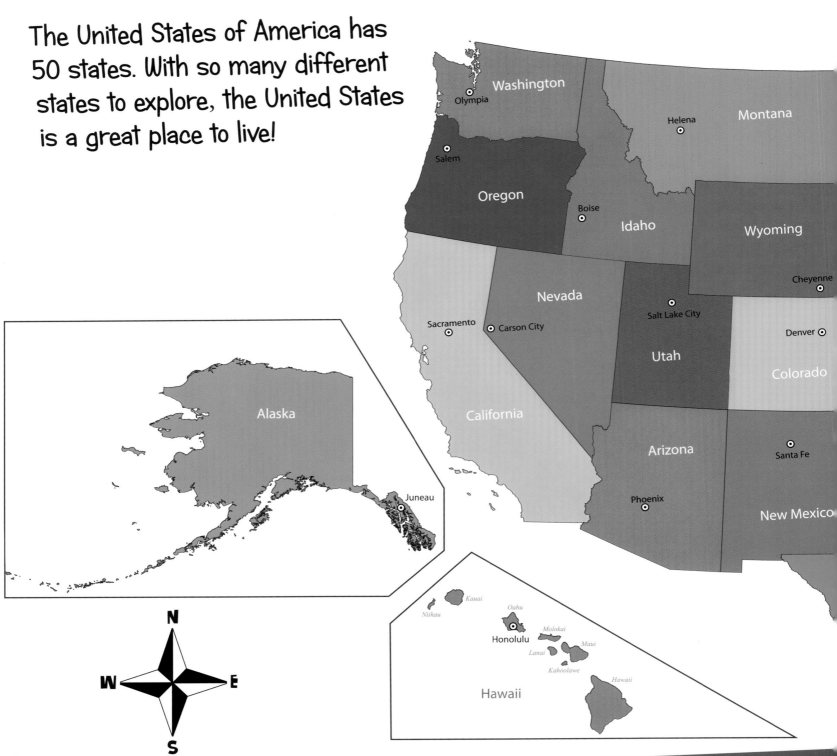

North Dakota
Bismarck ⊙

Minnesota
Saint Paul ⊙

South Dakota
Pierre ⊙

Wisconsin
Madison ⊙

Michigan
Lansing ⊙

Maine
Augusta ⊙

Vermont
Montpelier ⊙

New Hampshire
Concord ⊙

Boston ⊙ Massachusetts

New York
Albany ⊙
Providence ⊙ Rhode Island
Hartford ⊙ Connecticut

Pennsylvania
Harrisburg ⊙

Trenton ⊙ New Jersey

Iowa
Des Moines ⊙

Nebraska
Lincoln ⊙

Illinois
Springfield ⊙

Indiana
Indianapolis ⊙

Ohio
Columbus ⊙

Annapolis ⊙ Dover ⊙ Delaware
Maryland
Washington, D.C. ◻

West Virginia
Charleston ⊙

Richmond ⊙

Kansas
Topeka ⊙

Missouri
Jefferson City ⊙

Kentucky
Frankfort ⊙

Virginia

Raleigh ⊙

North Carolina

Oklahoma
Oklahoma City ⊙

Arkansas
Little Rock ⊙

Tennessee
Nashville ⊙

Columbia ⊙
South Carolina

Atlanta ⊙

Mississippi
Jackson ⊙

Alabama
Montgomery ⊙

Georgia

Texas

Louisiana
Baton Rouge ⊙

Tallahassee ⊙

Austin ⊙

Florida

The Big Picture

The United States declared its independence from Great Britain on July 4, 1776. As a nation, the United States is known for freedom and opportunity.

government

the group that makes laws, rules, and decisions for a country or state; the U.S. government is a constitution-based federal republic

federal republic

a kind of government with elected officials at both local and national levels

capital

the city that is the official center of government in a state or country; the U.S. capital has been Washington, D.C., since 1790

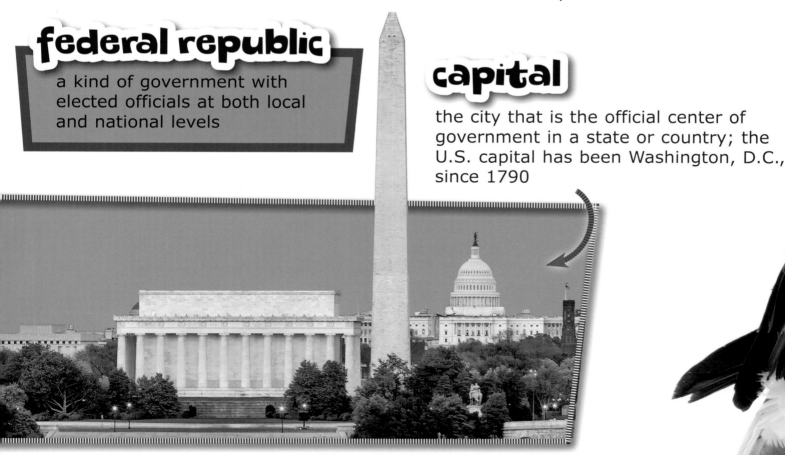

anthem

a national song; the national song of the United States is "The Star-Spangled Banner," written by Francis Scott Key

U.S. Constitution

a document that describes the basic form of the U.S. government and the rights of the people

independence

freedom from the control of others

symbol

a design or object that stands for something else; the U.S. national symbol is a bald eagle, which represents strength and courage

People

The United States was created on the idea of freedom for the people. Every year people from around the world make the United States their home.

population

a group of people, animals, or plants living in a certain place; the population of the United States is more than 315 million; California has the most people, and Wyoming has the fewest

Wyoming

ethnicity

belonging to a group that shares the same physical features, beliefs, or backgrounds; the U.S. ethnicity is 72.4% white, 12.6% black, 4.8% Asian, 0.9% American Indian and Alaskan Native, 0.2% Native Hawaiian and other Pacific Islander, 6.2% other, and 2.9% mixed race

language

spoken or written words; human speech; in the United States, 80% of citizens speak English, 12% speak Spanish, and 8% speak a different language

immigration

the act of moving to another country to live permanently; about 40 million people from other countries are living in the United States

naturalization

(nach-ur-uh-luh-ZAY-shun)—the process of giving citizenship to someone who was born in another country; since 2008 more than 600,000 people from other countries have become U.S. citizens every year

religion

a set of spiritual beliefs that people follow; the religions of U.S. citizens are 78.4% Christian, 4.7% other religions, 16.1% unaffiliated, 0.8% unknown

Government

The United States has a tradition of democracy. Every four years citizens vote to elect the president. Many people who work for the government must be elected to their jobs by the people.

Branches of the U.S. Government

- **executive**—the branch of government that the president oversees; it makes sure the laws of the country are followed
- **legislative**—the branch of government made up of the House of Representatives and the Senate; the branch that passes bills that become laws
- **judicial**—the branch of government headed by the Supreme Court; the Supreme Court interprets the U.S. Constitution and explains laws

president

the highest elected job in a class, business, or country; the leader of the United States

democracy

government by the people; a form of government in which decisions are based on people voting

federal government

the central government of the United States

Congress

the group of people chosen to make laws for the United States; made up of the House of Representatives and the Senate

Regions and Territories

The words "region" and "territory" are used to describe areas of land belonging to the United States. The 50 states can be divided into regions. A United States territory is an area of land, air, or sea the United States owns outside of the 50 states.

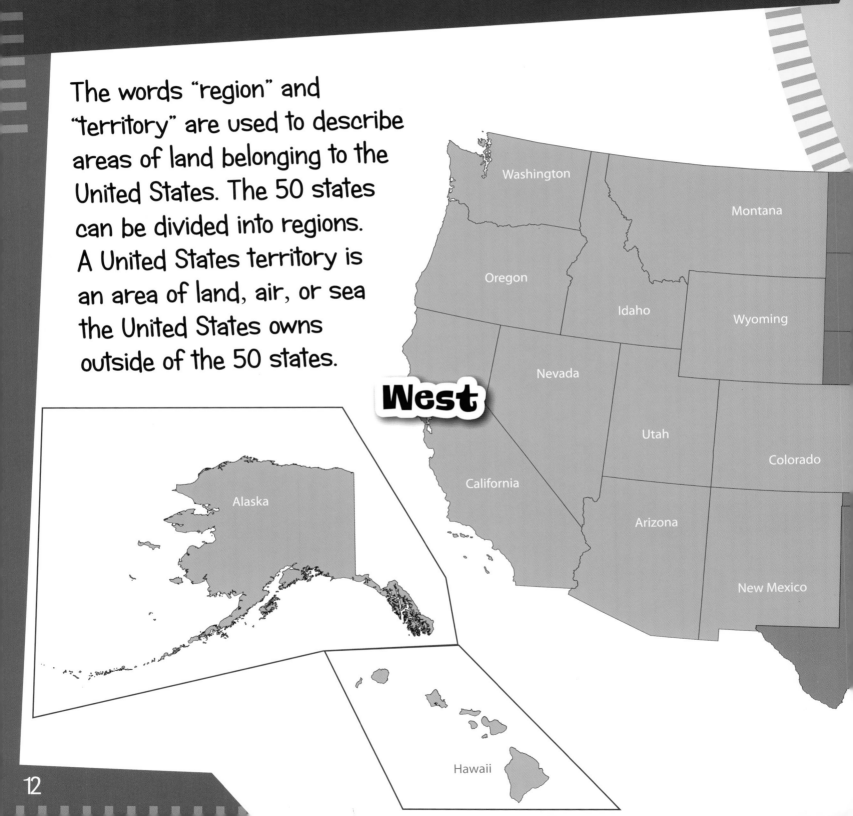

West

Washington

Montana

Oregon

Idaho

Wyoming

Nevada

Utah

Colorado

California

Arizona

New Mexico

Alaska

Hawaii

territory

an area under the control of another country; territories of the United States include American Samoa, the Federated States of Micronesia, Guam, the Midway Islands, the Northern Mariana Islands, Puerto Rico, the Republic of Palau, the Republic of the Marshall Islands, and the U.S. Virgin Islands

U.S. Virgin Islands

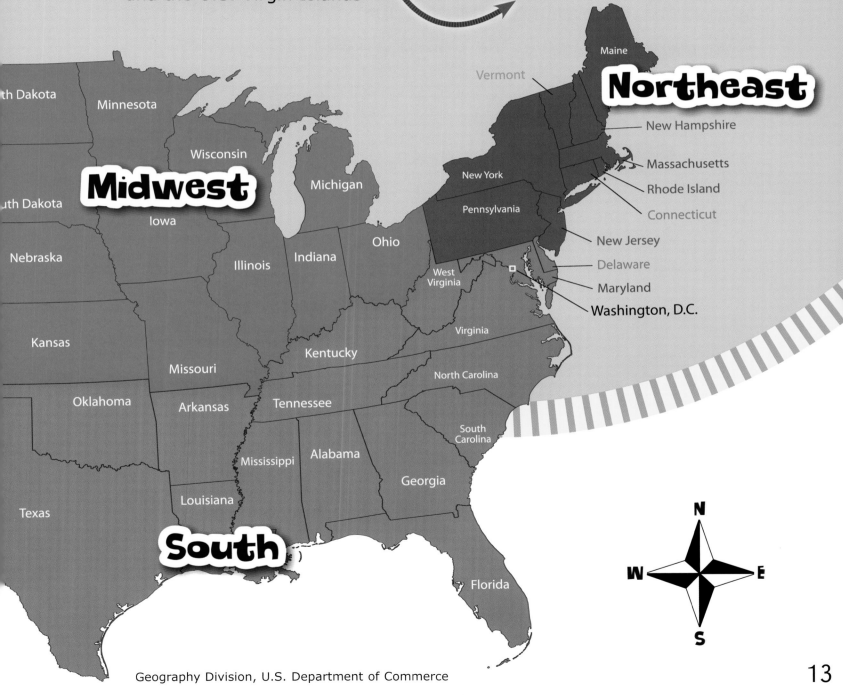

Maine

Vermont

Northeast

th Dakota

Minnesota

New Hampshire

uth Dakota

Wisconsin

Midwest

Michigan

New York

Massachusetts

Rhode Island

Iowa

Pennsylvania

Connecticut

Nebraska

Illinois

Indiana

Ohio

New Jersey

West Virginia

Delaware

Maryland

Washington, D.C.

Kansas

Missouri

Kentucky

Virginia

North Carolina

Oklahoma

Arkansas

Tennessee

South Carolina

Mississippi

Alabama

Georgia

Texas

Louisiana

South

Florida

N

W E

S

The Land

Every surface of Earth is either land or water. The 50 states are more than 90 percent land. But whether you're climbing a mountain or planting a garden, the land is different everywhere you go in the United States.

geography

the study of Earth's surface, its land and water features, and its people

sea level

the average level of the surface of the ocean; it is used as a starting point from which to measure the height or depth of any place

area

the amount of surface within a given boundary

natural resource

something found in nature that is useful to people; U.S. natural resources include coal, copper, lead, molybdenum, phosphates, uranium, bauxite, gold, iron, mercury, nickel, potash, silver, tungsten, zinc, petroleum, natural gas, and timber

U.S. Geographic Facts

area—the United States is the third largest country in the world; 3.5 million square miles (9.1 million square kilometers) of land

biggest state—Alaska, 571,000 square miles (1.5 million sq. km)

smallest state—Rhode Island, 1,045 square miles (2,707 sq. km)

highest point—Mount McKinley (Denali) in the Alaska Range is 20,320 feet (6,194 meters)

lowest point—Death Valley in California is 282 feet (86 m) below sea level

Mount McKinley

Mountains and Plains

The Great Plains run from north to south down the middle of the United States, where much of the land is flat. The Rocky Mountains tower in the west, and the east has the Appalachian Mountains.

divide

a ridge of land that separates two areas that are drained by different rivers

Continental Divide

Rocky Mountains

mountain range

a string of mountains that forms a group

plain

a large, flat area of land

landform

a natural feature of Earth's surface

volcano

a vent in Earth's surface that sometimes sends out hot lava, steam, and ash; Mount St. Helens in Washington is an active volcano

valley

an area of low land between hills or mountains; valleys often have rivers flowing through them

Major Mountains and Plains of the United States

- **Alaska Range**—400-mile (644-km) mountain range in Alaska; has the highest mountain in North America, Mount McKinley
- **Appalachian Mountains**—series of mountains about 1,500 miles (2,414 km) long that stretches from Alabama to eastern Canada

Appalachian Mountains

- **Brooks Range**—700-mile (1,127-km) mountain range stretching west to east, from Alaska to Canada
- **Cascades**—a mountain range that stretches from British Columbia to northern California; it includes the active volcano Mount St. Helens
- **Rocky Mountains**—a mountain range that stretches about 3,000 miles (4,828 km) from British Columbia in Canada to New Mexico
- **Sierra Nevada**—a 400-mile (644-km) mountain range that runs along the eastern side of California
- **Continental Divide**—a ridge that follows the Rocky Mountains running north and south across North America that separates the flow of water; water on the eastern side flows to the Gulf of Mexico and the Atlantic Ocean; water on the western side flows to the Pacific Ocean
- **coastal plain**—an area along the south and southeastern coast of the United States; it has mainly flatland and forests
- **Great Plains**—covers one-third of the United States, between the Rocky Mountains and the Appalachian Mountains; mainly flat, treeless land

Bodies of Water

The United States is bordered by the Pacific Ocean, Gulf of Mexico, and Atlantic Ocean. The 50 states are home to many rivers, lakes, and streams.

ocean

a large body of salt water; the Pacific Ocean is to the west of the United States; to the east is the Atlantic Ocean

sea

an area of salt water that is part of an ocean; seas are usually partly enclosed by land

lake

a body of water surrounded by land

coast

the land next to an ocean or sea

Great Lakes

a group of five connected freshwater lakes that lie along the border between the United States and Canada; they are Lakes Superior, Michigan, Huron, Erie, and Ontario

river

a large natural stream of freshwater that flows into a lake or ocean

gulf

a part of an ocean or sea partly enclosed by land and usually larger and deeper than a bay; the Gulf of Mexico borders the southern United States

bay

a part of an ocean or lake partly enclosed by land

Mississippi River

Major Rivers in the United States

Columbia River—flows from the Rocky Mountains in British Columbia into Washington and Oregon, before ending in the Pacific Ocean

Colorado River—begins in the Rocky Mountains and flows into the Gulf of California

Mississippi River—begins in northern Minnesota and flows all the way to the Mississippi River Delta, where the river meets the ocean, in the Gulf of Mexico

Missouri River—starts in the Rocky Mountains of Montana and flows for 2,341 miles (3,767 km) to St. Louis, Missouri; the longest river in the United States

Ohio River—flows from Pennsylvania to Illinois; it is one of the largest rivers that flows into the Mississippi River

Rio Grande—flows from Colorado to the Gulf of Mexico; it is 1,900 miles (3,058 km) long

Climate

Tornadoes, hurricanes, and blizzards—the United States has a huge range of weather conditions. Whether you're sweating in Death Valley, or freezing in Alaska, you are sure to find an extreme!

climate

the average weather of a place throughout the year

tornado

a violent, spinning column of air that looks like a funnel; tornadoes touch land and can destroy anything in their paths; the United States averages more than 1,000 tornadoes a year; most occur in the states of Texas, Kansas, Florida, and Oklahoma

temperature

the measure of how hot or cold something is; in Death Valley, California, in 1913, it was 134 degrees Fahrenheit (57 degrees Celsius), the highest temperature ever recorded in the United States; the lowest temperature ever recorded in the United States was in Prospect Creek Camp, Alaska, in 1971, when it was -80 degrees F (-62 degrees C)

blizzard

a heavy snowstorm with very strong winds; the United States averages about 11 blizzards each year

hurricane

a strong, swirling wind and rainstorm that starts over the ocean; also called a typhoon or a cyclone; about five hurricanes hit the U.S. coastline every three years; the peak hurricane season runs from about mid-August through October

National Parks

The United States has 400 national parks. Delaware is the only state without one. Known as the president who helped protect wildlife and public land, Theodore Roosevelt established five national parks during his presidency.

Grand Canyon

made up mainly of the Grand Canyon, a mile-deep valley of the Colorado River that is more than 200 miles (322 km) long; the park spreads out over almost 1.25 million acres (505,857 hectares) in Arizona

Acadia

made up of a group of islands on the Atlantic coast in Maine; it is home to Cadillac Mountain, the tallest mountain on the Atlantic coast

Great Smoky Mountains

includes more than 800 square miles (2,072 sq. km) through the southern Appalachian Mountains in Tennessee and North Carolina; it's the most visited national park in the country

Yosemite

(yo-SEH-mih-tee) a park in California, in the Sierra Nevada, a mountain range in eastern California and western Nevada; known for its waterfalls and giant sequoia trees; it spans about 1,200 square miles (3,108 sq. km)

Rocky Mountain

a park in Colorado that is in the Rocky Mountains; more than 60 peaks in the park are higher than 12,000 feet (3,658 m)

Olympic

a park in Washington that features the Olympic Mountain range; it takes up nearly 1 million acres (404,686 ha)

Yellowstone

a park mainly in Wyoming that stretches into Montana and Idaho; the first national park in the world; the Old Faithful Geyser is its most popular attraction, but it also has canyons, forests, waterfalls, and lakes

Zion

features sandstone cliffs and red canyons; Zion Canyon is the main attraction of this park in Utah

23

Landmarks

A landmark is an important building, structure, or place. The United States has more than 2,000 national landmarks.

Golden Gate Bridge

designed by Joseph Strauss, the 1.7-mile (2.7-km) bridge in California connects San Francisco to Marin County

National Mall and Memorial Parks

landmarks and museums near the Capitol in Washington, D.C.; they include memorials to Abraham Lincoln, Martin Luther King Jr., and Thomas Jefferson

Statue of Liberty

a national monument that has stood as a symbol of freedom on Liberty Island in New York since 1886; France gave this statue to the United States as a gift; it stands 305 feet (93 m) high and holds a torch

USS *Arizona* Memorial

a structure in Pearl Harbor, Hawaii, that marks the spot where the USS *Arizona* was sunk in the attack on Pearl Harbor in 1941 during World War II; the memorial is dedicated to the 1,177 servicemen who lost their lives during the attack

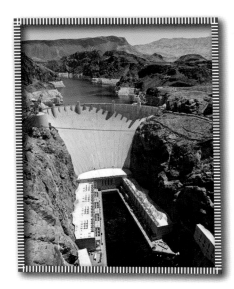

Hoover Dam

named after President Herbert Hoover, this dam is on the Arizona-Nevada border; the huge concrete structure is 726 feet (221 m) tall and 660 feet (201 m) wide at its base

Independence Rock

during the 1800s this large rock in Wyoming was a landmark for people following the Oregon, California, and Mormon trails; over the years many people carved their names into the granite rock

Mount Rushmore National Memorial

a sculpture of the heads of presidents George Washington, Thomas Jefferson, Theodore Roosevelt, and Abraham Lincoln carved into the side of Mount Rushmore, near Keystone, South Dakota; the heads are 60 feet (18 m) tall and took 14 years to complete

Quirky Tourist Attractions

The United States has many beautiful and historic places to visit. You can also find places that are "off the beaten path." Check out these places for something fun and different!

Jell-O Gallery

a museum in Le Roy, New York, that holds many Jell-O items, from oil paintings to gelatin molds and magazine ads

World's Largest Ball of Twine

a ball of twine in Cawker City, Kansas, now weighs nearly 10 tons (9 metric tons) and is at least 40 feet (12 m) around; in 1953 farmer Frank Stoeber began rolling his extra twine to start this massive ball

Enchanted Highway

a 32-mile (51-km) stretch of highway just east of Dickinson, North Dakota, that features scrap metal sculptures of pheasants, geese, deer, and more alongside the road; the sculptures were created by local artist Gary Greff

Roswell

a small city in New Mexico that is famous for an alleged UFO sighting and crash in 1947

Carhenge

38 cars are arranged in a circle on a plain in Alliance, Nebraska, to look like Stonehenge in England; created by Jim Reinders

Corn Palace

a building in Mitchell, South Dakota, that has a wall covered in pictures and designs made out of corn kernels; each year the pictures are replaced

Biosphere 2

a center near Tucson, Arizona, that features a 3-acre (1.2-ha) enclosed research facility for studying Earth's ecosystems

Cadillac Ranch

an art display in Amarillo, Texas, that was created by Chip Lord, Hudson Marquez, and Doug Michels to make local citizens wonder; 10 Cadillac cars are buried nose-first in the ground

State Flags

Do you know what your state flag looks like? Each state has its own flag, and each flag uses colors and symbols to represent that state.

 Alabama

 Alaska

 Arizona

 Arkansas

 California

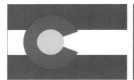 Colorado

 Connecticut

 Delaware

 Florida

 Georgia

 Hawaii

 Idaho

 Illinois

 Indiana

 Iowa

 Kansas

 Kentucky

 Louisiana

 Maine

 Maryland

 Massachusetts

 Michigan

 Minnesota

 Mississippi

 Missouri

 Montana

 Nebraska

 Nevada

 New Hampshire

 New Jersey

 New Mexico

 New York

 North Carolina

 North Dakota

 Ohio

 Oklahoma

 Oregon

 Pennsylvania

 Rhode Island

 South Carolina

 South Dakota

 Tennessee

 Texas

 Utah

 Vermont

 Virginia

 Washington

 West Virginia

 Wisconsin

 Wyoming

Fun Facts

Want to know more about the United States? Here are some fun facts. What do you know about your own state?

First State to Join the Union
Delaware joined the Union December 7, 1787.

Last State to Join the Union
Hawaii joined the Union August 21, 1959.

Most Professional Sports Teams
California has 21 pro teams in basketball, baseball, football, hockey, and soccer.

Longest Main Street
Island Park, Idaho's, main street, on Highway 20, is 36.8 miles (59 km) long.

Makes the Most Maple Syrup

More than 1 million gallons (3.8 million liters) of maple syrup were made in Vermont in 2012.

Tallest Building

The Willis Tower (formerly known as the Sears Tower) in Chicago, Illinois, is 1,451 feet (442 m) tall.

Longest Cave

The Mammoth Cave System in Kentucky is more than 390 miles (628 km) long.

World's Smallest Park

Mill Ends Park in Portland, Oregon, is just 2 feet (61 centimeters) across.

Read More

Allen, Kathy. *The First Independence Day Celebration.* Our American Story. Minneapolis: Picture Window Books, 2010.

Eldridge, Alison and Stephen. *Mount Rushmore: An American Symbol.* All About American Symbols. Berkeley Heights, N.J.: Enslow Publishers, 2012.

Juarez, Christine. *The United States of America.* Countries. North Mankato, Minn.: Capstone Press, 2014.

Titles in this set:

Show Me **COMMUNITY HELPERS**

Show Me **THE CONTINENTS**

Show Me **DINOSAURS**

Show Me **DOGS**

Show Me **INSECTS**

Show Me **POLAR ANIMALS**

Show Me **REPTILES**

Show Me **ROCKS AND MINERALS**

Show Me **SPACE**

Show Me **TRANSPORTATION**

Show Me **THE UNITED STATES**

Show Me **THE U.S. PRESIDENCY**

Internet Sites

FactHound offers a safe, fun way to find Internet sites related to this book. All of the sites on FactHound have been researched by our staff.

Here's all you do:

Visit *www.facthound.com*

Type in this code: 9781476501178

Check out projects, games and lots more at **www.capstonekids.com**

32